Facts About the Secretary Bird

By Lisa Strattin

© 2016 Lisa Strattin

Facts for Kids Picture Books by Lisa Strattin

Anaconda Python, Vol 11

Angora Rabbits, Vol 12

Blue and Gold Macaw, Vol 13

Brown Recluse Spider, Vol 14

American Coot, Vol 15

Spix Macaw, Vol 16

Blue Catfish, Vol 17

Burrowing Owl, Vol 18

California Sea Lion, Vol 19

Capybara, Vol 20

Caracal, Vol 21

Chuckwalla, Vol 22

Hyacinth Macaw, Vol 23

Sign Up for New Release Emails Here

http://lisastrattin.com/subscribe-here

Join the KidCrafts Monthly Program Here

http://kidcraftsbylisa.com

All information in this book has been carefully researched and checked for factual accuracy. However, the author and publisher makes no warranty, express or implied, that the information contained herein is appropriate for every individual, situation or purpose and assume no responsibility for errors or omissions. The reader assumes the risk and full responsibility for all actions, and the author will not be held responsible for any loss or damage, whether consequential, incidental, special or otherwise, that may result from the information presented in this book.

I have relied on my own observations as well as many different sources for this book and I have done my best to check facts and give credit where it is due. In the event that any material is used without proper permission, please contact me so that the oversight can be corrected.

Table of Contents

INTRODUCTION

Secretary Bird is a huge bird compared to other normal birds we witness in daily lives and it has some very unique characteristics and appearance. Also it is globally known as the bird of prey. Usually found in open grasslands this bird has two major colors in whole body, the grey color which runs from the head down to the belly and the other black which covers the tail, wings and legs.

COLOR ME

Other than that it has beautiful and attractive red circles or outlines around the black iris eyes and a crown shaped feather set on the head that is followed down until the outer neck. The overall appearance of Secretary bird is highly appealing. As it is a grassland bird that too in the prey category so it has long legs that keeps itself a little higher from the ground in order to look around for any new prey and also to save its life at the same time by being aware from prospective danger.

COLOR ME

SIZE

The general height of Secretary birds is 1.3 meters that is almost 4.3 feet; they are large enough to be recognized easily. The Secretary bird can look like an eagle for once although the long legs cast a distinct image of it. It has an eagle like head with a hooked bill and well-rounded wings that are strong enough to take higher flights. The wingspan of Secretary Bird is about 191cm to 220 cm and the average weight could range in between 2.3 kg to 5 kg and till date the highest body mass is recorded as 4.02 kg somewhere in Southern Africa.

COLOR ME

The average tarsus of the Secretary Bird is 31 cm and the tail is around 57 to 85 cm, these both factors collectively make it look longer and taller than the other species of raptors (birds of prey like eagles and hawks). The neck of the bird is not very long; it can only be lowered down to a particular level, because after that the birds have to stoop down to the ground to drink water.

COLOR ME

HABITAT AND BREEDING

Most commonly the birds are found in the open grasslands and savannas instead of forests and dense shrubbery areas. Commonly the Secretary Bird can be found in the Sub Saharan Africa and its range is extended from Mauritania to Somalia and to the south of the Cape of Good Hope. This is a non-migratory bird and likes to be stagnant to one habitat generally but in the case of searching the prey and favorable living conditions the species has shown some migration patterns. Otherwise there is not a specified pattern for the migration of Secretary Bird in winters or summers.

COLOR ME

For breeding the Secretary Bird use the nests that are built at a height of a minimum 16 to 23 feet on Acacia tree, and almost around half a year before the laying of eggs male and female Secretary birds visit the nest. The incubation period of eggs is around 45 days, after getting hatched for about 40 to 60 days both male and female feed the young ones. Generally, in Secretary bird there is no concept of sibling aggression but the youngest one out of three does die due to starvation. Almost at the age of 80 days the young ones are able to fledge and jump out of the nest in the controlled environment. After fledging the parent pair teaches the younger ones tricks to attack and get the prey and soon the younger ones become independent.

COLOR ME

SOCIAL BEHAVIOR

Secretary Bird is not that much of a friendly or socially active bird species as it belongs to a hunting family. Most of the time the pairs could be witnessed helping each in bringing up the younger ones and also incorporating others in the flock in order to maintain a stable equation among them. On the other hand, it is also perceived to be an aggressive bird when it comes to fighting. Secretary birds have shown to give a brutal time to the opponent and also adopt some of the amazing body transformation that simply showcase all the anger and rage through its actions.

COLOR ME

DIET

Secretary Birds hunt down their diets from the environment and surroundings, and the common food intake is of insects or mammals ranging from mice to hares. In addition to that mongoose, snakes, lizards, tortoise, young birds, bird eggs, crabs and sometimes the dead grass animals too are the part of the diet. The bird is not really very selective in food trends, generally it depends and eats based on the availability of the things at that time and it likes to grab everything in the moment. The hunting strategy that the Secretary bird uses in case of dangerous and poisonous reptiles like snakes is very effective and prompt as the bird attacks upon the animal in a sudden moment and snap the neck or back by the help of its feet that makes the prey lose the fight.

COLOR ME

SUITABILITY AS A PET

Having the Secretary Bird as pet is really not a suitable idea; as it is a free bird that chooses to live in a free and open environment. Having it at a limited place with controlled conditions could be a little difficult for the person as well. In the natural conditions the bird lives through a natural cycle of hunting and survival and some things in nature cannot be replaced.

COLOR ME

It will be really not a good idea to have a hunter at one's place as pet that could also threat the life of the other pets or animals around you in the general environment. Mostly, you can witness the Secretary Bird at the grass lands in an open environment with the unlimited land where it can roam and air dive to any extent. Due to the resemblance with the eagle family it does have some of their traits, and thus to have it as a pet you are required some of the skills and expertise in handling it.

Please leave me a review here:

http://lisastrattin.com/Review-Vol-30

For more Kindle Downloads Visit Lisa Strattin Author Page on Amazon Author Central

http://amazon.com/author/lisastrattin

To see upcoming titles, visit my website at LisaStrattin.com – all books available on kindle!

http://lisastrattin.com

SECRETARY BIRD PUZZLE PRINT

You can get one by copying and pasting this link into your browser: http://lisastrattin.com/secretarybirdpuzzle

KIDCRAFTS MONTHLY SUBSCRIPTION PROGRAM

Receive a Box of Crafts and a Lisa Strattin Full Color Paperback Book Each Month in Your Mailbox!

Get yours by copying and pasting this link into your browser

http://KidCraftsByLisa.com